ELEANOR AMONG THE SAINTS

Rachel Mann is a priest, writer, theologian, and broadcaster. She has written fourteen books of prose, criticism, poetry, and theology. Her poetry has been highly commended in the Forward Prizes for Best Single Poem and is widely anthologised. She is a well-established radio broadcaster and regularly contributes to BBC Radio 4's *Thought For The Day*. Currently she is Archdeacon of Salford and Bolton in the Diocese of Manchester, UK.

Eleanor Among the Saints

Rachel Mann

CARCANET POETRY

First published in Great Britain in 2024 by
Carcanet
Alliance House, 30 Cross Street
Manchester, M2 7AQ
www.carcanet.co.uk

ISBN 978 1 80017 381 1

Book design by Andrew Latimer, Carcanet
Typesetting by LiteBook Prepress Services

The publisher acknowledges financial
assistance from Arts Council England.

CONTENTS

ELEANOR AMONG THE SAINTS

PRAISE

A CHARM TO CHANGE SEX

ELEANOR AMONG THE SAINTS

ELEANOR AMONG THE SAINTS

'Therefore I must be intimate with you, and lie in your bed with you. Daughter, you greatly desire to see me, and you may boldly, when you are in bed, take me to you as your wedded husband...'
– *The Book of Margery Kempe*

EMBROIDERING A PRIEST

In the beginning, hem and line of thread,
A tug, a song of praise, arms raised orans-wise
Sanctus Sanctus Sanctus
Let those with ears hear: Love and love.

Before he enters Sanctuary, I shall speak
Direction of twist, all those loops whipped, corded,
Doubled and open, thrill of flounce and picot.
I stitch him slow, so slow

He doesn't recognise his nearness to completion,
He shall appear *ex nihilo*, blessed with cordonnet, beautiful
Embellishment, if only he knew my skill,
Such relief, my talent. When he raises Host

He I we shall be complete, he will forget (we all do)
The mysteries of his making, a birth. He will be
All flounce, a skin, layers of bride mesh,
He shall know folds.

SUBSTITUTIONS

For seam read rip
For stitch read thread

For rip read stitch
For thread read tear

For tear read notion
For button read hole

For notion read button
For hole read dressed

For dressed read bare
For scared read cut

For bare read scared
For cut read tears

For tears read rags
For scraps read all

For rags read scraps
For all read all

ELEANOR, IN THE BEGINNING

Sew me, sew me weird, stitch me fingers, teeth,
My lids and legs too, sew me new, together/
Apart, stitch me skill and fright,
Sew me not dolly, not plaything, but monster,

Thing of nightmare, all agency, free finally of what
You'd make me; sew me into escape, O
God of thread, shoddy, scrap – You know, you know
Text is textile texture textus,

You know all conjugations, the parts and trips of speech,
All fibres of the Book, the stitching and snipping,
All ways a world gets from there to here.
Assemble me kind, assemble me wild,

Read me insane and lovely and never afraid of clash.
Unpick me old, spin me a yarn worthy of queer –
I am story queen, myth mad weirdo;
Like the rabbis say, make me *masekhet*,

Loom me into Law, woven from readings, discards,
I do not care for making sense, I could be all schmattology;
Construct me dress, show-off, fucking *haute couture* –
As if I were Scripture, Tanakh

Worthy of that much care,
Construct me weird and kind, leave it to me
To strip off when I'm ready. I shall run wild,
Naked as I dare, out into sober streets.

ELEANOR CONSTRUCTS A FATHER

'Call no one father on earth, for you have one Father'

Heaven's a bore. A hallowing on earth, I shall work
Grammar, my will, his hers ours, your will, mine,
Enflesh in mouth till speaking's bone, blood, pulse;

If only, lip-magic! if only word worked that way for me,
Though if I bear Image too, why not hallowing be mine?
No. Sorcery's for Jesus, mud made miracle, his brave translations:

Dadda, daddy, dad, I doubt he really knew you, Pater Noster,
Out past Dadda, out past all the hand-me-downs, past
Child's first trembling question: Why do adults call fear 'love'?

ELEANOR'S BOAST

Hear me. I am bite of first Black Apple,
Eden's pearmain that was Worcester sent,
I saw Devil's bright arms drop his Spittleful,
Great gob of slag on Wyre – Nightjar eggs
And badgers' setts, nighttime economy

Smeared under tons of brim. I'm witness to
His dazzling gait, I saw smoke of His fall,
His burnt-out wings, the stumps of near-divine
Trembling between His shoulder-blades. I saw
The marks of St Michal's spear on His chest.

I am garden. I knew St Kenelm, boy-king,
In my acres, I showed him truth of love:
There's no sin when you're laid beneath earth,
Only a split of seed and a slick
Of underway, the germ of tree and root.

Listen! I'll tell thee, tell, tell-tale… I
Am Ellie of the Cut, Factory Fortnight Queen,
I am the undredged. I lurk, old trollies, I
Am pike, the flash of jaw in oily depths –
Stour and Severn flow in me. I break your lines.

Out on Kinver Edge, they name me Beast,
I am sighted; I am lope of half-seen,
At Witch's Tree they carry out their sentence.
Parson, I am the arm of rustics crabbin' thee,
I am bereaved earth, can you hear me yet?

ELEANOR DREAMS

Boy again: gangles, spider legs, all elbow and joint, I'm shrunk,
I cycle capillary, body-map, my own, my own BMXer tricking
The Pipes, all red, a festival of oxygen and iron, my teeth

Blackened edge-land; through long miles of vein I go,
No end, will there ever be end, there are centuries of cells,
Archives of self no one will ever see, and still on, pedal, no god –

I am near clogged; O Mary of the long miles, pray for me;
Grant space enough, O Christ of the flowing blood.

ELEANOR AMONG THE SAINTS

IS IT A SURPRISE

That those who force sticks down their throats
Yes you, Cat, you, I see you and know
Is it a surprise that I've learned the meaning of bodies
The holy angels the cherubim and seraphim
Burn my lips with coals, selah selah
Is it such a such a surprise, Cat
That all I know of bodies I know from you?

For bodies read flesh, read meat, for meat read delicious
Contradiction, we don't know what they can do
Or what limit is, *taste Jesus taste even the nails of his toes*
We know not limit except in the test, *let me test you Cat*
Let me think of what it must feel like to taste
Bark, bark on palate, a stick on tonsils
No one made you do it Cat, did they?

I am almost too scared to try, I have tried so many things
Most alien and kind, I am so scared, since when
Did that stop me? I dream of sticks, of ash and oak
Birch elm
Would willow tickle not hurt
Beneath my mind are twigs, cast-offs
Of tree *terror*, I dream

I have seen fear and hope
Let me in love, you know I care, not so different
For you Cat: *Jesus take me now* before I gag
I dream that the bite, necessary and sufficient, that my lick
Will make him disappear, *the Divine,* broken departed
And when he finds his way out (*Do you even know me Cat?*)
He shall be a tiny god lost in underworld

I HAVE COME TO ACCEPT

That salvation has cruelty inscribed
Into its honey-sweet new day, *Katherine. Yas queen*
Ain't that a fact. Cruelty is one way to say God –
Think Abraham, a ram and near-knifed son, *does anyone*
Recover from a god like that? Consider Christ
Himself, his beating, world without end

But you, Katherine, you light up the sky
Born as the Wheel dies, *all glory be,* oohs and ahhs, crowd
What did you feel like to be translated into saint?
I think of blades, *what language can you hear,*
I think of blades, their grace as they fall, and crowd,
Fifty thousand. A little boy points, his smile

Perhaps you were already beyond, beyond *Katherine*
As blades fell, already. *What language do saints speak?*
As a child I cheered when we carried you through streets
Everyone's pin-up, yas queen, I ready to be knifed for glory's sake,
Magno gaudens gaudio, rejoice you company of boys.
Come Katherine make of me, my parts, make me

ONCE WHEN I WAS YOUNG

I was shown Dauerwunder, *Love's harvest in a vial*
Liquid and bright, *shred of you, your blood,*
Perpetua, word without end, *thou lasting miracle*

Grant me forgiveness, sister, *brother, Pet.*
I get lost in words, their syllables, forget their moral point
Oh, *Dauerwunder,* enough to see your shape written down

Naked on page, all lovely words become porn
Dauerwunder, oh to trace your triphthong, to taste you, tongue
Does that make me the worst kind of sinner, Pet?

I would smash vial for you, feel you on hands
Priest of the Sanguine Mysteries, Perpetually
I would travel with you, Pet, into arena, *witness lover friend*

I shall be more than *lasting miracle* –
Loss of breast, of vulva vagina. Womb. Loss of hips, loss
O Reliquary. I shall witness grace, its works

A change in light and fact, a change, Per pe tua
For all time, Pet, your body refined, liquid and bright
I could be reliquary too, not man not woman, not end

ELEANOR CONSTRUCTS A MOTHER

Every last forsaken placenta, you. You –
Every flood between between every woman's legs,

Mamma, make Eve clean, me too, mamma
You present in present, a priest's song, memory;

Who flowed, a belief, in water from side,
Wound of Him, do you pray still? *nunc et in hora*

Mortis nostrae. Memory is night-terror, so better
Off to forget, though dream is all festival, *ave ave,*

Queen of Heaven, in dream every street is flowers, bells.
Smoke of love rises to your celestial home;

I carry you all days, every day, mamma, dig you
Into my shoulder-blades, you fill my veins,

O Queen, can you feel my burn? I've seen statues cry,
Aren't you glad? Lift me, a heaven, as I carry you.

AQUINAS ON BEING

'Because a small error in the beginning grows enormous at the end' - Aristotle

he who is Husband swived me, licked me,
ne villein ne knave but Free-Man wived and swived me,
I hold testimony, a nesting of truth in heart, breast, belly,
my Soul swells to Clean-Mother in heaven, her girl.

no error: a Free-Man, a very Jesu, nimbed me, nimbed me beautiful,
y'cram thy belly, he said, *till Apple-gorged, y'cram thy guts
with babee, and let dug squirt, till bell of heaven stynt. I believed.*
I too a fullness/emptiness, like woman beshitten at birth,

or man qualmed. I can be fullness, if Him a fullness, if Him
shining with Divine yet bread, substans accidens
I too a wiving, all sacral, hymen bust, and if not seen as such,
at least in version You made, a fabling. Like Rood, I'll lodge in dream.

ELEANOR AS JULIAN AS MARGERY

Hazelnut and tears, a meaning of I –
Consider the curve of salt water, its dribble
Down face, I am all meniscus holding back
The edge of edge and others might say ugly,
I say holy, I swear there is nothing more beautiful
Than a face under pressure. Nothing more
Like hope and hazelnut, and last hazelnut
Survives and shews the eternity, goodness
As the red of raw, face as worst of winter,
World without end. If I do not make it to tree,
Not even sapling, my sealed-up body, my fury,
A sufficiency, more than enough, universe is tears.

ELEANOR AS A SIXTEEN YEAR OLD MURDERED TRANS GIRL, WHAT IS KNOWN

Safe is a conditional
Natural is easy oh so
I am not restricted to your version
You did not need to know this

I am already subject to edits
I am the scene of a break-in
Requiem is Vigil
Matter is a word with multiples

I am struggling to rise I am all my own breath
I am not code for another's sins
You will recall my joy
My joy is not a substitute

I did not know a body could be killed multiple times
I think this might be one such attempt

ELEANOR AND ROLANDINA IN THE CITY OF GOD

'And I saw the holy city, new Jerusalem, coming down out of heaven from God' Revelation 21.2

1.

Ald and Bishop, Moor and Cripple, Alder, New and Lud, gates traces walls, refrains, an earth music; now we're out, out past death, I hear it, how Romans tramped trampled, and I remember when I was young there were still temple traces, half the churches recycling, traces of traces, temple as rubbish dump, a warning that even empires, especially empires get rubbed out, even empire of ones and zeroes, even flow of money, it's all flame and gutted in the end, a fire music, even flesh sex fuck, all romance, even Love, undone. I hear them: bombs, sweet lip-whistle as they fall, an air music, I see bombs fall, bombs are hidden too and River not enough to sooth a wound of City, hush of water song, as for me – even Risen – I am overwhelm; I want want to see past glass, concrete, towers, shew me when is glass not sea, crystal sea, empire turned to tree, zero, one, I want, I do not want. Dina, Dina, will that do?

2.

Eleanor, I admire this talk of Love, of universe out beyond mortal death,
Out past that death which isn't death, past love, time short as breath
In wrecked lungs. But can we get on with other things, risen things?

There's so much to get into one another, beyond breath, air, beyond
Money, more than transaction. I want to know if this is how Christ felt
When he was rammed back into limb, face and neck, after wreck.

El, we have wonder, the thisness of what bodies become beyond scar, wound,
Beyond use and fuck, even the best of fucks, we have the sheer shine of
Rise Up. And, El, if this is risen-ness indeed, then it's cast-off too –

Noli Me Tangere, and I shall be wash-clean, their hands, oily confidence,
Trace of garlic and ale, their breath, the itch of hemp on neck, gallows
   and cheers,
The eyes, appraising eyes, always appraising, *is she all she seems, what's she*

Prepared to do, stained as canal, their hands all on you, me. How long the rope
To clean break her neck, all that: now past care, gone.

3.

My point, El: even if only in grease of finger, a palm smeared, desperate
    window stain,
Even if only stomach emptied in alley, and slick of condom,
Here somewhere, beyond river turned sewer and centuries crushed, all
    those streets
And other Englands lost, all the polyglot made clean in zero and one, and
    plague bodies
Limed, a certainty: City of God. And it's here, it's here and everywhere
    here, raised –
The City, no mere economy (though never doubt mysteries of money, it
    gets into everything),
All lovers know it might get into them, zero and one, and maybe
That's okay, tolerable anomaly; but we are Jesu now and the Raised don't
    Consume

4.

Oh, Dina. Once there were so many cities.

ASH WEDNESDAY

'The gathering of the ashes is a protest against arbitrary power' –
Gillian Rose

Eleanor as Phocion's wife, out beyond City, *khora khora*,
Eats ash of husband, all that is left, body as excommunication;

Taste of it: rot of fruit beyond rotting, lily and latrine,
A choke of throat and tonsils gone black, mourning past dust.

Eleanor as Phocion's wife, she looks up, City inescapable,
Columns, marble white, beauty, tyrant; what is left?

We brought nothing into world, we take nothing out,
Not even Eleanor, she knows psalm: sins I have committed

Against thee are more in number than sands of sea,
Will mourning become Law? Eleanor as Phocion's wife,

Athens is all temptation. Her body aches, charred body,
Perhaps that is Love's taste grown old. Eleanor out beyond City,

Oh, Eleanor, run, run. She stands, death mouth,
Love, that bruised attention, barely begun.

If I, such as I, am ever allowed Lyric, its tender inflections:
Poem as near dawn, winter soon, mist not ready yet
To abandon earth and gains of night, festival of cliché –

If (I am all conditional), then it will be England again,
Villages still asleep, I shall drive into Sundays of words,
Preachers and songs, psalms soon to speak of God safely

As if He no longer punishes, as if He long abandoned
Clay and blood and fire as medium for love's making
And love's murder, as if Body discarded;

As if 'natural' was still a word that grips
A world, as if that word could name what is, all Adam,
My kind mere rumour, gossip. I too, a Cain, would kill for love.

BLOOD SPORT

Panic of Lyric, panic, she (always she) flees towards edge
Of page, but nowhere to hide in wide white margin, and edge,
Oh that edge, mouth-dried limit, precipice, heart-burster. Nowhere
To hide, that's the problem with poem, it stands out black from white

It does not wish to disappear, but be sung, a stand-out,
Folk song: a fox fiery with cunning or hart still mistress of the ridge
Dares stalker to fire fatal shot, his ship, fate of the world, becalmed.
That's the problem with poem – all drool, near feral, frightened

Of being ignored, and oh her secrets, the secrets she keeps
Secrets she casts-off, the chase, false trails that smell the best –
Comma, colon, ellipsis stenched with seminal fuck, pheromones
For the unwary, and best, the best of it: there are no false trails.

Parson knows, he knows that my Redeemer liveth, and
I shall stand at latter day upon earth, and though,
After skin, worms destroy this body, yet in my flesh
Shall I see God. O God, do you also believe?

I do not mind, I have grown accustomed,
I have laid me down to earth a dozen times, been Raised
Why should not I prepare for marriage with you?
I have shed tears enough, and sin, I am not so strong

On words, what is Sin? Even Jesu knew limits of Truth,
He shewed value of a life, I should like to learn from that,
It is so difficult to judge what is alive when
You are surrounded by the dead. Perhaps parson

Is right: there is a City yet to come, though body descends
Skin and skin, all failed evolution. He says, I hear a voice,
Heaven, saying unto me, Write, From henceforth blessed
Are the dead: they praise thee, they rest, they rise.

ELEANOR AS WIDOW

The LORD will destroy the house of the proud: but he will
establish the border of the widow. (Prov.15.25)

Comfort me, oh comfort me, a world, all world,
Grant me world in card solicitously given, acres
Of white, gold, a forest of sympathy, stiff universe,
A mantelpiece, behold! And a priest says

Some wounds never heal, tears are the price of love
The best cliches, and, yea, Lord will destroy the house,
All world dried to rings of spilled tea, rings –
Small planets, cold, and borders shall never be crossed.

Eleanor, a version of you, near the Fall, *Queen StripNaked*:
Behold! Layers thrown-down in street, coat of fox and wool,
Leave Hunt and Shepherd Work to other gods – Artemis, Jesu –

Let public gawp. *It's just her, him, gemaeden! Miltestre!*
Abandon hat and houpellande in pool of piss and ice,
You are skin, you are sleet burn, you are Epiphany,

An eye-feast, a Sovereign at work. Prise off sheets of self:
Epidermis, dermis, O Doctor, let out sub-cut fat; work lunellum,
Remember you too are vellum ready to be written on.

Be joy of saint, be Mary taking sex into heaven, all grin, all teeth,
Body as catechism: lung for love, heart for promise, gut for compassion
Behold! St Peter Cheap where you first tasted God –

Now Queen, now Goddess, now Eleanor, now
You are question: where might the future begin?

PRAISE

'God in your goodness, give me yourself'
– Mother Julian of Norwich

PRAISE (1)

World as in all things, and universe unspoken, unsayable,
Of which no end, world without, world without end,
And world also a single breath, the unseen, water gasp,

Heat leaks into and out of lungs, a song, a song;
A birdsong half sung half croaked, magpie at sunrise.
That is a kind of prayer, *is* prayer, yes? I pray.

I pray my beads, a priest, I pray them, each a world
Each decade the last, pray, seek, breathe; Oh, trust Unseen City,
That gasp of water, heat, it cries for its dead, all Yes.

ASH WEDNESDAY IN THE CITY OF GOD

I smear a greasy cross again, again,
Behold! A Cross glistens on a people's heads
And soon I shall stand at the Gate, a hope boundary,

Rain as cold as fire, our only defence an umbrella;
There are wolves within, sheep without, and a City
Truly exists only within, corruptible and vast.

Perhaps youth is holier than old age, thus:
Lord — not yet! Lord, Lord, Not Yet. A City
Grows within, perhaps I am Rome after the sack,

Gardens burned, the laughter, the screams, jewels
Scattered in the street. *O Lord.* I, priest smeared,
Cannot see the Body, incorruptibility. What's that?

A MORNING PRAYER

Another city, a city of glass and tall tales,
So many bodies blurred, vehicles stretched,
A breaking point, all the half-hidden faces

Recede in rear-view mirrors, and what was once
Shall never be again, small and smaller,
Till earth abandons tarmac, forgetful. Soon, trees

Spread canopy, a longing, and I say, *O Lord*
Open thou, O Lord, I wait. Someone, someone somewhere
Makes response, surely: *And our mouth, Thy praise.*

Shew forth possible, O Lord, on all days
And on this day too, let grace fall between branches,
Let prayer, and if I were ready to make peace

I could claim gun-fire, a farmer scaring rooks perhaps,
As psalm, so much liturgy, a mother laughs, her child.
O Lord open thou our lips, a beginning, and morning

Requires long-tried words, new day held in old,
Stress laid on stress, a test: *The night has passed*
And day lies open before us.

DAY OF RESURRECTION

Beyond glass, as it should be: Behold! a church rises
Above garden and fence, Behold! a theatre of brick and sacrifice,
Work of pulley and hand, Love of centuries made tall.

But I no more than Mary must cling, *noli me tangere,*
I can hear bird – whistle and whoop, mating call an alleluia –
I can hear song above technology (headphones, unmute, *cue in 3,2,1*).

If I must leave Church locked, I shall be Study, piles of books,
Words and words, and Word: *He is Risen!* supposedly, He is, He IS.
Can I believe without sight of candle, feast, first flame?

I find a/the Table where I can, gather splash and fragment,
Wheat, wine, all the sureties He left behind, and the inescapable words:
This is my body, this is my blood. I need no witness, seen,

Though grant me unseen, sparrow and blackbird, magpie and wren,
A single car, a hush as it passes the front door; grant me vision:
Men and women who still run away in wonder, awe.

PHYSICIAN HEAL THYSELF

The Lord be with you, and my mask slips from nose
Flood of sweat already and no sign of People
As in the days before before, when

Eating, drinking, marrying and giving in marriage
Until the day that Noe entered into the ark, and knew not
Until the flood came, and took them all away;

I hear only masked and muffled sound: *And with thy spirit.*
I shall trust as best I can: we are people, People of God, though
Would it matter if we were not? Bodies have always been

Divers creatures, carriers of understandings, Sin
In skin and particle of breath, perhaps we have become
Colonies for unseen, whole armies march through.

WHITSUN

That Whitsun, I was early, priest in search of what if, back behind God in
flames,
Back behind dying Faith (noise and drums, the quickening of a dance),
that Whitsun
A search, a search, and I drive towards church for Word unyielding:

Dearly beloved, all things requisite and necessary, and as many as are here
present,
Trees are bunting red white blue an abundance, a joy perhaps, a plague?
I don't know how to discern, and now houses are turned flag too, flimsy
and ragged in wind,

The roads are flags, I am flag, and Lord hear me: *we have erred and strayed*
like lost sheep;
I conceive this a Preface, this drive an offering, a ride into horror, pastoral,
an old film:
Soon I shall wear my crown of flowers, prepped for pyre, a comfort, a
beginning.

HUMBLE ACCESS

But thou art the same lord whose property is always to have mercy
And soon I shall distribute You on tongues. Property is also building, is
Brick, is mortar, public, behold! All shall see and many shall enter.

I shall trust in manifold mercies, and if flesh bread, if blood wine
Then why not breeze block? Let teeth chew mortar of God,
From grit to grit thou art, and it is good very good, concrete, such

Salvation. Maybe we are all plaster saints now, washed clean –
As if paving stone, let secrets sink beneath, a burial,
And ever more, we shall dwell in him and he in us.

COMMON PRAYER

All Summary, all reminders too (*Lay not up for yourselves*
Treasure, rust and rust and moth), all beseeching and oblations;

I kneel as another Priest dines on feast: *O Lord, O Lord,*
of thy goodness and in this transitory life trouble, sorrow,

Need, sickness, we bewail manifold sins and wickedness.
I am famished, forgiveness bloats my belly,

And comfortable words flake my tongue, it has been so long
So long since creature of bread and wine,

And for such a time as this, O Merciful Lord, grant us;
I step forward, approach the Altar, a supplicant,

Priest drops God into my palms, God bathes my alcohol hands,
I'd forgotten Creator, Redeemer could be so light, an intoxicant;

I clasp Him tight, I carry the Universe back to my Stall,
A flesh reliquary. I eat alone, this is feast, I lick God from my palm.

have mercy on us; seven bodies, met in vastness, and a god is sleeping, back of the boat, so Gospel says, a god is sleeping and invites trust as another storm rages. Water bursts wall and roof a steady song: *times up times up*. And thou that takest, Lord, have mercy, have mercy on us, we too a building, and this is home; a god is sleeping, or laughing, or tells a woman off for asking help, domestic, dares to say her sister has chosen the better part; thou that takest, thou, O storm God, takest away the sins of the world, have mercy, or let us sleep or laugh too. Home becomes rain and flood and time is up, a god is sleeping. A priest holds the Paten, three pieces of Kyrie untouched.

AN EVENING PRAYER

Tonight, I shall be tell-all, tell how outside
Became mine, mine again, how glass
Of eyes misted and I learned breath,
O Physician heal thyself.

I shall tell all, of blue, of old roads
As if newly-laid, Jerusalem, blue of bluebottle,
Gleam of rain, who knew pavement
Could raise a body through shoe?

I shall be tell-all, hear! I touched
Neighbour's wall, *Love thy Neighbour*
As thyself, tip of finger tap, this is God
On first day in Eden, first things felt –

I did not know tree, mere sight, could be Jesu,
I am tell-all, like He who was raised
He sings Day we cannot dare yet see.
Tonight, I speak a hymnody.

PRAISE (2)

December, season of impossible and hope absurd
(*watch O Mortal for Return, god made small in birth*),
And I try again 'praise poem'. Why, I hear an old poet friend say,
They exist only to make fools, he should know,
I've seen the failures, words all over his study floor, a flood in ink;

Why try now, as I hide in my mother's room and I see,
Of all things in December, a butterfly on the windowsill
While downstairs dad struggles to get his breath. Butterfly.
That's a mockery of time if ever there was,
What the hell are you doing here in this season of squelch,

Only tremble of proboscis a giveaway that whatever alive
Means for you, you are that. Butterfly, unlocked from chrysalis,
Tricked by a centrally-heated age, the house ever hotter
As dad's arteries freeze; or maybe this is simply a ruse of God:
I saw a red admiral once, air-dancer, in church

As we said requiem for a youth, it was metaphor (obviously),
But also beauty in fact, flash of wing, resistance to gravity of tears,
That was praise. Dad is still downstairs and he is freezing up,
Every breath a fight against encroaching ice age, a new age
Past old age, a time of glaciers, and I should go to him,

Embrace what can be felt of love in a season of frostbite,
And together, perhaps, we shall seek praise, even in such an age
As this when time itself fails, and perhaps if he could still
Get enough air to speak he might answer the question of praise:
Why does a body struggle on, drag the world in

Through fog and chill, finding just enough to force it back out,
Why butterfly now? My fantasy, a fear: because it's life, he says,
And this is all I have left and of it everything is wonder,
Even the purgatory of ice age, even the edge of breath on tip
Of tongue escaping from me, and all worth, and everything is praise.

For my father

you were never shepherd, border-wanderer, indifferent to wall
and dyke, but if the flow and ebb of your life had drawn you
there, you would have found stillness, a true use of crook at
the wild edge of things, who sinks shaft in earth. Whose very
silence is call, who knows that to be staff sunk into dirt is to
transmit truth, a gift of tuning, humility itself another way
of speaking earth, and body and staff a voice heard beyond
hearing. Behold! Flock stirs, raises mouths from grass, cud-
jaws dropped low, ears dripped with winter and all eyes a
search for twitch of trouble; trust now a matter of how rain
marks out a body as tree and tree as body, a matter of water
rolling from crook as if love itself had found a final shape, a
tune as it taps on coat and boot, jacket and hat, as if wind
and water held a secret speaking, and earth knew all places we
have ever been and ever shall go and somehow all things are
humus-child, the old ram finally remembers, he walks towards
you and flock follows suit.

DOMESTIC CHAPLAIN

Night, and exhaustion lead me to cliché: swirls are roads from toe to heel, via,
And nails, once white as milk now yellow, curled crust of clotted cream.
Skin too, brittled with age, split, an unloved leather, heel creviced
Where mites might delve in search of god.

Near ankle, ooze. I touch brine, sea and ocean, and flesh as bloat,
I lift one foot, move it to plastic bath, one then the other, lift and lay it down.
It's okay, dad. I hear you groan and know you are creature of earth
Not sea, a boulder-man, I too want to trust these feet

Again, great scoops of planet which have buttressed more lives
Than your own. I lift them and lay them down as if they were newborns,
Pause and say, *it's okay, dad*, his flinch as his heel
Touches lukewarm water. *It's okay, dad*, it's okay, to be sand.

FEAST OF THE EPIPHANY

A version of the slow lane, traffic and traffic,
Trolley for car, walking for seated, men and women,
A version where vehicles have wheels that spin
In all directions, my left front wheel spins and spins;

I have words – *grapes, bananas, two skimmed milk,*
Two bleach – I have words, a liturgy, and here aisles
Have no vergers to act as guide, no established convention,
Which is a kind of freedom; so I press on, spin and spin,

No one speaks, no one waits, no one says A Thing,
No cantor, all responsorial absent, I clutch my words
And I do not say A Thing. I look for gaps, slip
My trolley in close to cheeses I cannot eat, I stare at taboo

And a woman stares at me, does not say A Thing,
This must be stare as hurry-up, this is what passes
As aggression, as morning prayer at this hour; alcohol
Not reserved for Sacred Purpose, the walls are brown

And green with it and the drinking yet to start.
This is mask time, all snoods and neckerchiefs,
Concealed noses, all the half-faces, and I think we might
Have been desperados once, we too were raiders,

The banditry of youth or something, and I repeat
The words I was given, *grapes, bananas, two skimmed milk,*
Two bleach, I set them alongside words offered back
By this place – *exotic, three-for-two, chilled items* (i-tems –

Who uses such a word?), *twenty percent off, twenty percent*
Less plastic, how I am intended to react?
I could cheer, salivate, spin, but no one cheers or salivates, or
If they do, they do so privily, privacy of heart, and anyway

Grapes, bananas, two skimmed milk and two bleach,
That is all I need, just the basic brands, nothing fancy,
But goods from all the world are gathered, all places, all times,
World, Word, and so much flesh, meat presented professionally,

That's reassuring; it's the reassuring thing about meat,
Parcelled up in such a way that no one could ever believe
It will breathe again, revived to field, to chew cud, low,
Stare with loathing. Still, there is no sufficiency,

Perhaps, that's it: I am here to remember heartfelt,
So when my mother asks what was it like I can shrug, say
'Well, I was so glad to get out of there', grapes etc.
A pleasing adjacency, an adjacency of Word.

BURIAL

A crow feasts on crow, black banquet, and I approach Door;
I am here to receive corpse and a line, a line arises,
'He cried with a loud voice, saying to all the fowls that fly

In the midst of heaven, come, gather yourselves together
Unto the supper of the great God', a benediction;
Take flight ye rasping Word of God, go in search of Kingdom

While omens idle, and if war and rumours of war,
If I can no longer lie down to sleep without vision of light,
Burn of broken atoms, if in dream I am skin, boils, all trauma

Truly I am also Door and at Door for another end.
Corpse, beloved Father,
Come quickly, set me to task, a crow feast. Even if
The world ends tomorrow, still, still I would plant the apple-tree.

PRAISE (3)

mappa mundi, that's a kind of praise, behold! cities of salt, brimstone rivers,
Christos Pantokrator heals the scorched edge of world into dream and

if I, Priest, were source of praise, that is where I would be called too: a world
with all my sin and hope razed/raised, behold! Cain remembers the feel of fist

on cheekbone, black pulse of blood against skin, skin on skin,
behold! vellum gathers vein and membrane, my body's frayed fibres

massed into myth, and all my beloveds – mandrakes, the Cinnamon Bird,
blemmyeh, Mary Redemptrix, all the models for a life, Buffy and Jael,

Tiresias, Eleanor – swarm, a testimony; and a god, his steely throne
his angels made ink, blurs of tattoo, a triumph (judgment?) etched in beast

FYLDE COAST APOCALYPTIC

Of all ends (fire, ice, pale horse), none of the predicted.
Rather: a house, seashore, a room
Sealed by brick and glass, glazed, mirror-dim.
A house, warm and bright, walls of hydrangeas,
Acres of white and powder-blue, and out beyond, a view –
Beach at low-tide, sea sucked out, grey as whale.
Out beyond, banks of sand and pools cling, I hear no sound,
Further still, surely, raw waves crash,
And rain's venom. A nursing-home near the end (attendants gone,
Tea stains and cake crumbles, silent TV), and out beyond,
A partial witness: man with rod, he runs towards the swell,
Casts and waits, he's no fisher of men. No need
Of me. And me of him? Earth curves beyond sight
And close to its edge, venom rain, miles and miles.

A CHARM TO CHANGE SEX

Of all that God has shown me
I can speak just the smallest word …'
– Mechthild of Magdeburg

A CHARM TO CHANGE SEX (1)

After Anglo-Saxon Charms

Male male,   excrete of male,
Not in war bones   not brick sweat
Callus of long days   or tree-felling
But sent north   to tundra, earth scorch
Where slick of body   every last spume of you
Milked clean   stain on ice
Sweetly black it goes   out past purple the good death
Into mother mother   reset, the born again
Bone marrow stripped fresh   ready for filling
A cast off, unnecessary   all afterbirth, first body, truth
And dream, child, dream   forget, not quite

SEVEN PROOF TEXTS ON A TRANSITIONED BODY

1.

One version: a migration,
Cells and molecules, all mine, all the bitter code
That chains-up to make a life, become cloud

Of birds lifted up from strip-clean, a field;
Moved by lean demands of hunger,
Urge to be elsewhere, that old fury

In cortex, hippocampus, bird-brain of shortened day.
I've known air change in lungs, drop in pressure,
Gasp, some hangover of reptile which demands

Salt, warmth, a dry continent of self.
So, a migration, then. That's the word, cool
With science, able to hold the facts of body

When gene's compass tickles and pulls.
Or if not science, a phenomenon known.
And if somewhere you've only travelled in dreams

If somewhere you've never been,
Then what of that other field?
Stripped now, but perhaps. Winter. Spring.

2.

'Every woman who makes herself male
Will enter the kingdom of heaven,'
Says one version of Christ.[1]

What, then, of the male who makes
Of himself a woman?
I am awake again, 4 a.m. and from out

Beyond window: orange-yellow stain of new day
Seeps beneath curtains. Dying streetlight,
Or afterglow perhaps, all wars all climate ends

Come to fruition at once and all that is left to me:
Wait for the roar, sound-barrier crack
To catch-up, suck out breath;

Inside, just time enough to note other things:
My good pissing days are long gone, if I were a river
I've dried beneath the dam; I toil on toilet,

Title my study: 'The body undressed.'
Premise: the penis does not yield to prayer.
Evidence: Lord knows, I tried;

A childhood wasted in petition:
Lord, grant me serpent skills, that old magic,
Version of Easter Day – new body raised, slough,

Out of old, another skin; Cut out depth of voice, and
If it be profitable for thee that one of thy members
Should perish, hell postponed, if thy cock offend, selah.

---

1   The Gospel of Thomas

3.

Suppose answer to prayer is a captive:
Girl of the deep. When I was a child I prayed

As a child, thought as a child, *Oh girl of the deep*
Hide me in thee. Let us descend

To thy dwelling-place, Persephone, shew me dwelling,
Seek and ye shall hide, hide me in thee

Among the abandoned: *Professor Plum, Mrs White,*
Stretch-Armstrong, mounds of Desert Rats, Afrika Korps,

Smashed trucks, my war crimes, all of childhood's dead.
I will lay me down, snuggle in decay

Girl of the deep shew me what November means,
Shew me Hades' tricks – night by night

We'll rot in silk and frills, rubbish-dump
Queens, we'll never stir, we'll never make a sound,

Together in secrets, together in prayer –
Our prayer, a supplication: *oh god, please.*

4.

Awake at 4 a.m. and conclusions to be drawn:
As Eckhart says, we are meant to be mothers
Of God, we birth him as we can, not as we ought;

Thus, I assert the absence I made between my legs
Is mystic: an initiation into secrets, sealed eyes,
Sealed lips, nighttime is for mystery and song –

Cry me a river, oh *piss me a river*,
What say you, Meister? I hold you in hand,
Paperback mystic, I hold all your quotes, speak:

When the soul is downcast then it is called woman;
When it recognises God it is man. A hairy-balled soul,
Then, is for the best, but I know body undressed,

The body undressed cannot lie, it is annunciation,
Its own: *Behold, I shew you mystery*
We shall not all sleep, but we shall all be changed.

5.

A child again, school to be faced, *the Lord's my refuge* –
And Eve, Lilith, Mary Blessed One, all our mothers
Even – especially – my own know the only question,
A thousand times asked, every inflection:

Sometimes, barely a whisper, a wren at distance
Pleads for bread, or thick with tears and too much
Coffee, another night in search of satellite in the dark.
There is a version in a garden (of course) –

Orchard of laden trees, fruit is offered, her voice
Sweet as Eden before the Fall, till it breaks off, full-stop,
Unable to swallow yet another of my sins. Sometimes,
She begins to begin, that first syllable too much, trembled plosive

Shakes apart. There is the film, the one where she sits on my bed,
Doctor to her patient, and I pause rewind play pause
As she reaches the comma, careful intake of breath, between
There's something I want to ask, and point of no going back.

6.

A version of childhood in which *girl* is the original word
World's first day, light/dark, separation, a dove hovers
As the universe expands and *Word was/is with God.*

Book and sentence, all books, all from one sweet syllable –
Source of Eden, Lilith's cry. Her fuck you. All cries. *Girl.*
New bones, clean lips, wrongs unpicked.

7.

Awake at 4 am, and young again,
Scars erased, self-portrait as Jesus
Before the scourge (Thesis: only the young
And untroubled truly know the delight
Of God); a body yet to be settled,
Back in hospital for the final step.

They're trying to kill me, Oh God,
They want me dead, an old lady's shout
From across the Bay, perhaps even
From that other shore, that other light
Oh Comfort ye, comfort ye, my people,
Dare I speak my response?

Sweet Holy One, Mother listen: Body, body
Drains away into plastic, transfiguration is fluid –
Yellow, red, brown; bags of liquid God, *pierced one,*
He bears our smell and stain: *he bore our sin.*
Holy Mother, let us be translated
Into constituent parts. Do not be afraid –

If *world without end,* then glory too and
If glory then all our loves, all cries, longing,
For all things are held in You.
Glory be to the venflon, and to the saline,
And to the catheter, *world without end,*
Amen, amen, amen.

A CHARM TO CHANGE SEX (2)

Iron-child, rust	embrace, speak a rusting
Speak, speak	speak a rusting
Steel skin pit,	pit, a blackhead, skin turn blue black
Hell-child, flake	rust and flake, red, to an autumn,
Give you layers to air	fall, embrace what is left,
Mere core, mere pip	glow! charcoal, mere memory of God,
Molten, o glory	flesh shucked of bag that held you
Be you screamer	for end and love
Be you bones	a new thing prepped,
Be you	a finding, find you fat and curve,
Fat of tree, sap	fat and curd, a springtime of meat
Be you a tearing	tears too, know blood in new places
Word never same	a crash a cramping be you
New-found	no more stenched with boy

AFTER

Best I can suggest: heart-judder – *outdoors* after plague,
breath a bonfire of tyres, a dare unmasked and I don't care,
all temporary versions of soul dropped to earth, litter.

Or space of poem, maybe, a walk into gaps where words won't go,
Not even pronouns. Everyone limps, but no one accepts they're wrong,
That's one way to talk of love, love of oneself, God I barely know;

Shouldn't seeds fall and sprout? That's the way of ordinary things,
I've witnessed bodies move on street in park in garden they fall.
Best I can suggest: hearts beat and unbeat, and glory is, glory is, mine too.

DELETED LINES

No need to explain, Pater Noster:
True names are found a way along, deep in.
Start with hand-me-down, comfort of orphans, comfort,
Rat-earred doll. Let me parse you, till mine breathe –

O Pater Noster, they'll dice for your tits
It will be for keeps when they wipe you out,
They'll chew your bones, but still you'll long for something –
Some damned bitter grace, even when the facts are plain.

It's not your fault and yet it is always you;
I've seen statues cry, all is miracle, yet you never miracled
Me. Oh well, the world is an exquisite poem set off
With antithesis. Who wrote that? O Lord, Seal-Breaker,

The Lord and King of Ash, blot out my sins,
Quench me in oxbow, if there are rivers here,
Jordans to be crossed, silky with spring rain
And world without end till the end of all. Here's

The thing: One can kill for love –
I believe that, so do you, I think we all do,
Why else legislate against it?
Why else sharpen a knife? Oh, Love, sweet love.

DECADE OF PRAYER

Devon August 2022

1.

Gull, no matter how far gull flies (land-fill, black-bag, bin-land):
Twinge of sea, lick of salt, wave, a dream, that's a kind of memory;
Surely, tell me, and can swallows lose their way?
I think so. If thrush were stormed out
Past shoreline, an ocean, what of home?

2.

I'm still a Learner. Teach me, God, if you, you old tick and habit,
Teach me, not mere mask and masque, or reaction, reactions;
Teach me: a search for memorable, a marker.
Save me from tombstone.
When they find my bones, erase me from thy sight.

3.

I walk lanes, and First Principle: I am never alone.
You seethe in horsefly, I kick You up, dirt and stones,
Sparrow cracks free of bramble, flees; always You,
Uncomfortable words. Community is holy, right?
Just once abandon me, O Christ, make me wonderful child.

4.

I walk lanes, see corpse – orange guts, a spew of juice and pips,
Orange flows into slick of green, a fruiterer's beast, mostly rind;
Plastic for skin, bin bag black, shredded,
All anonymity gone. I should like
To claim this thing, a new species. If not I, then who?

5.

I find my way to Church, spire is compass of love,
And inside the door: Font. Birth then, a stone birth;
Identity has depth, and conversion
Is experimental, suggests Weil. Also:
'Society is the cave. The way out is solitude.'

6.

Later, a beach, scraped clean, a planet's skin,
It might be scene after war, a film of war –
David Niven walks untroubled from spray after the Death Fall;
Sanderlings peck and walk, they know my secrets, I should follow,
I should like – spirit of cliché – to describe the waves as hush, a temptation.

7.

Am I lost now in myth? Soon, I find myself in Valley,
Below me sheep, above hawk, he keens, a scratch in sky.
Certainly, I am between, a path, oak and ash;
Here is my fantasy: I am last woman in earth, Eve abandoned,
Time to decide – turn back, all my lovely sins, or head on.

8.

Friends, not always unkindly, tell me sex change is impossible,
I say God, in God – nothing. God's stern power smites
Flat rotundity of the world, yes; I arrive at Bridge:
Road closed, follow diversion. There is a thrill of swallows,
The last thermal of summer, they dance, cogitate: air, continent, globe.

9.

Now I remember: there is a place in Hell called Malebolge,
Tiresias's final home. Arse about face, ditch of shit, a warning,
An invitation; Violet hour draws near,
Hell-mouth too, and I wait. I am not even lost,
But I would welcome a guide. Virgil only has time for better poets.

10.

Garden, and far off in the woods, a scream.
At last, no myth, merely children, a game of tig,
Tiralee tiralaah, deep in the forest they go; no bars, no Gs,
Not even E, a cut off. I should like to promulgate a decade of prayer.
Garden, God. I am so far from signal, I can't read me.

#TDOR

Will you, would you, would you please, would you please come,
We know, we really do know how busy you must, and it would be,
And season, season of remembrance too, only makes more powerful,
Amidst poppies and holy ones and time of shadow it only adds, adds to

Poignancy, re-membering, and the lads and saints and all dead
And this year we want to make it extra special so if you, and if not you,
Then could you suggest? We would want words, let there be words,
Just the right amount, perhaps you could shape, words and words,

And names, we shall read names, could you suggest
How we read names, so many, a day where sad and name
And list mean same, and some names the pronunciation,
But they matter don't they and you will agree and each year

The words and the names and the candles, it's our privilege,
A way to show we care for your, our community, our users asked,
And we shall go outside or we shall be outside already,
We have names, we got names from website, so many

And we thought, what do you think, in batches of ten,
We have readers, and we have you, of course, you could, if you would
Read some, Eleanor, El, Laurel, Bryce, Angel, Kyle, Angelica,
Eleanor, saints souls, such a season as this, St Eleanor St Kyle and you

Would you, perhaps you could say words about you, a story,
Say what it's like, what trans, what is trans, is that the right word,
And every year will you be present, a speaking Eleanor, El, Laurel,
Bryce, Angel, Kyle, Angelica, Eleanor, Jesus and we know we know

Names matter, matter to you, and to us and every year St Eleanor,
St El, Laurel, St Bryce, St Kyle Martyr, and ditch they say,
Ditch, that's where they found, a ditch, we want you present,
Please don't stop, there are candles and ditch, could you say words?

NIGHT QUESTIONS

To whom must they go, the little foxes, to say, "Take us, take us, that spoil the vines"?

What is this Nocturne that sounds in my bones?

If Blessed Virgin is mystic, more than alive too, what flesh is she?

How body and also Body?

When will I become bread, ever more wine?

Whose body, whose blood am I?

Will I ever find my way to the start of the World?

Am I a Satan, a prepper for day when I too shall fall?

What sin longs to define?

If Resurrection, then what of bodies – mites, bacteria – that flourish in mine?

Will you, whoever you are, make of me a shibboleth?

Will my end be Garden or Glass?

O God, oil-blacked bird, might you yet save me from World Without End?

A CHARM TO CHANGE SEX (3)

Nail, nail   a purpose: to bind, a breaking
Seal of soul   wood wound, that's a purpose,

Iron, blood, tree   bleak singularity organ and organic
All earth now   iron become meat made flesh

Word made verb   to pierce, parse it – break
And pound, pound   a pounding and somewhere

Hidden: transfix   oh so holy, words lead everywhere
Invisible made visible inside become out

Nail, nail   a tree splits, sap drips, wood is meat
And meat is iron   worthy of praise, iron-meat

Praise, pit-worth   dogs chew bones, mother weeps
A heart, absence   meat knows, meat knows not resurrection

ENVOI

If at the end, fabrication, so? All text is stitched,
Body too only subset of making, a stored magic –

Oxygen, nitrogen, carbon, carbon and trace and trace
Of trace, base and noble, transmutations, a gifting;

You too: recipient, a trace of trace, trans, queer, every name,
A mutate of Love, good and holy, trace of trace in you –

Trace of every name despite your best efforts, your horror.
No one and nothing so very far from embryo or Eden,

The wild play, from chromosome and myth, wondrous edits,
Additions, all of us hand-me-downs, a holy cause;

Behold! she becomes they, all worm-gorged earth, or bed worn
And wet with fuck, let us be lines sown into lines, a break.

Eleanor among the Saints

Eleanor 'John' Rykener (or John 'Eleanor' Rykener?) was a fourteenth-century seamstress, embroiderer and sex worker who has been claimed in recent medieval studies as an example of a trans person living in medieval England. There are stories of her working in both London and Oxfordshire as an embroiderer, as well as her working as a barmaid and a sex worker. The evidence we have of her existence is drawn from an interrogation by the Mayor of London which followed her arrest in Cheapside in late 1394 for having sex with John Britby, a former chaplain of St Margaret Pattens. Under interrogation she spoke of how John became Eleanor under the influence of Elizabeth Brouderer, an embroiderer and possibly a procurer of sex. Eleanor spoke of how she had sex for pleasure and for money with both priests and nuns. The scholars Ruth Mazo Karras and Tom Linkinen say this: 'We can say that even if we do not know anything about Rykener's self-identification, their life as a male-bodied woman was 'transgender-like'.' Was John/Eleanor Rykener trans in the modern sense? That feels a stretch. However, as I've reflected ever deeper on the meaning of being trans I've been drawn to Eleanor. She invites mythologizing. I've read that some say she never existed at all. That only makes hir/her/him more interesting. She has received, through the extraordinary energy generated by queer medieval history a most extraordinary resurrection. I guess my poems about Eleanor, written through imaginary versions of her – as seamstress, sex worker, as wife, widow and most of all as a near contemporary of medieval saints like Julian of Norwich, Margery Kempe et al – represents my own attempt at an imaginary archive.

The title poem imagines Eleanor in conversation with three saints: St Catherine of Sienna, famous for only being able to digest the Host of God (and who reputedly used twigs rammed down her throat to make herself regurgitate conventional food); St Katherine of Alexandria (the most popular saint in the Middle Ages) from whom we get the famous Catherine Wheel. The myth has it that when she escaped from the Wheel of Death when God made it explode, fifty thousand onlookers died; and St Perpetua, an early martyr of the church who reputedly changed sex from female to male at the moment of her death in the Roman Arena.

Eleanor, in the Beginning draws on the thinking of French feminist rabbi and theologian Delphine Horvilleur: 'Sewing is the ultimate activity, involving recycling, travel and transitions'.

Eleanor and Rolandina in the City of God brings Eleanor into a 'risen' relationship with Rolandina Ronchaia, a fourteenth-century Venetian trans sex worker who was put to death for sodomy.

Day of Resurrection was originally published on The Manchester Writing School website, as part of its 'Write Where We Are Now' Project in 2020. Versions of *Fylde Coast Apocalyptic* and *An Evening Prayer* were published on the Sarum College 'Lock-Down Poems' site in 2020. I am grateful to the organisers of the Kendal Poetry Festival, Verve Poetry Festival and the Church Times Festival of Faith and Literature for granting me the opportunity to road-test a number of these poems.